The Book of Dirt

Also by Nicole Santalucia

Because I Did Not Die (Bordighera Press)

Driving Yourself to Jail in July (Dead Bison Press)

Spoiled Meat (Headmistress Press)

The Book of Dirt

by

Nicole Santalucia

The New York Quarterly Foundation, Inc.
Beacon, New York

NYQ Books™ is an imprint of The New York Quarterly Foundation, Inc.

The New York Quarterly Foundation, Inc.
P. O. Box 470
Beacon, NY 12508

www.nyq.org

First Edition

Set in New Baskerville

Layout and Overall Design by Raymond P. Hammond

Cover Design by Nicole Santalucia

Cover Art by Deanna Dorangrichia

Author Photograph by Deanna Dorangrichia

Library of Congress Control Number: 2019947956

ISBN: 978-1-63045-065-6

America, the plum blossoms are falling.
—Allen Ginsberg

Virtue, Liberty, and Independence
—Pennsylvania State Motto

Contents

You Have Now Begun Reading *The Book of Dirt*   *11*

Notes from the Commonwealth   *13*

Keystone Ode with Jane Doe in It   *14*

Keystone Ode with Moving Violation in It   *16*

from The Book of Dirt   *17*

Keystone Ode with Lesbian Car in It   *18*

Red State   *19*

Notes from the Commonwealth   *20*

Keystone Ode with Overgrown Garden and Invasive
Species in It   *21*

Keystone Ode with Homophobia and Ground Beef in It   *22*

Bitchtown, Pennsylvania   *23*

Notes from the Commonwealth   *24*

Red State   *25*

from The Book of Dirt   *26*

from The Book of Dirt   *27*

from The Book of Dirt   *28*

Keystone Ode with Assault Rifle and Grocery List in It   *29*

Notes from the Commonwealth   *30*

Keystone Ode with Hot Sauce and Motor Oil in It   *31*

Bitchtown, Pennsylvania   *32*

Keystone Ode with Marianne Moore in It   *33*

from The Book of Dirt   *34*

Keystone Ode with *The House of Mirth* in It   *35*

Notes from the Commonwealth   *36*

Red State   *37*

Keystone Ode with Founding Father in It   *39*

from The Book of Dirt   40

Notes from the Commonwealth   41

Notes from the Commonwealth   42

from The Book of Dirt   43

Keystone Ode with Local Journalism and the
Associated Press in It   44

Notes from the Commonwealth   45

Red State   46

Notes from the Commonwealth   47

Keystone Ode with Visiting Hours in It   48

from The Book of Dirt   49

from The Book of Dirt   50

Red State   51

Keystone Ode without Jaywalking in It   52

Notes from the Commonwealth   53

from The Book of Dirt   54

from The Book of Dirt   55

Keystone Ode to My Wife after Reading Anne
Bradstreet at a One-Hundred-and-Three-Year-Old
Farmhouse   56

Notes from the Commonwealth   57

Keystone Ode with Litter and Exhaust in It   58

from The Book of Dirt   59

Red State   60

from The Book of Dirt   61

Notes from the Commonwealth   62

from The Book of Dirt   63 *from* The Book of Dirt   64

Keystone Ode with Prison Dinner in It   66

Notes from the Commonwealth   67

Keystone Ode with Despair and an Unmentioned

Avocado in It   68

from The Book of Dirt   69

Keystone Ode with Environmental Contaminants   70

Red State   72

Keystone Ode with #MeToo in It   73

Notes from the Commonwealth   74

Keystone Ode with Queer Skin   75

Keystone Ode with Businessmen in It   76

Notes from the Commonwealth   77

On First Having Read *The Book of Dirt*   78

For my wife, Deanna

You Have Now Begun Reading *The Book of Dirt*

and on the title page it reads: *the opposite of prostituting*
is when I learned how to read—it was like sucking a lemon.

I spit out pale yellow seeds, open the door to earth,
look out the window. All my gay symptoms

rally in the library parking lot where I swallow my name,
blindfold my votes, and line them up against the wall.

I go to the county jail where I teach women to write
their guts on styrofoam and cinder block and floor wax.

I write commonwealth and red state and ode on the edge
of disaster where clouds cast a shadow in the shape

of a knife—I cut the faggot-label out of my shirts,
slice open plastic bags stuffed with childhood

and grass clippings from a blue state.
This is the book where a gay girl is in another closet.

Where the doorknobs fall off and the queer goes for a walk
on a rainbow leash. I mosey from dream to dirt to dream

and see the jar of hallelujahs glowing on my nightstand.
The opposite of gay is a seedless lemon spiked

on a galvanized nail. There's a penny resting on my tongue,
or maybe that's the remnants of a dream I can't quite remember.

When I wake up, there's a giant bitter orange tree
flowering at the foot of the bed. Cold-hardy fruit drops

between my wife and me. We empty the jar of hallelujahs
and cross-pollinate citrus with survival. *We don't belong,*

says the fruit. *We don't belong* is the logic of other books.
We survive. We survive on the resemblance of other oranges.

Depending on ripeness, our skin peels and our blood deepens.
The sweet orange is not a wild fruit. The pomelo is its maternal parent.

Our root systems twist together below ground.

Notes from the Commonwealth

This is the letter I'll tear into three pieces for three angels to devour or three truck drivers to deliver to three different addresses. The letter I am not going to send is what I am when I reach for the mailbox while I stand in the backyard. I stretch for those coupons for frozen broccoli and pizza. I reach over wild onions sprouting between the bricks on my house. This is where I stand and write the letter I am not sending. Between the wild onions and bricks is where the god of gates and entrances lives; he has two faces. His two-faced head thuds in the dirt. One face spits out a worm and the other has chapped lips; both look for water or a word for thirst. I'm thirsty and hungry when I don't write the letter that I'm not going to send. This letter would have explained why I'm not a mother and what it's like to sit in each chair at the dinner table. This letter offers a cure for alcoholism, encloses fibers to braid a rope, and directions on how to use the rope. Tie it around your ankles and sing if you want to run. Wrap it around your neck and jump if you want to relive all the pain. This letter has children in it that will never grow up. Three or four kids that share the family name. These kids are from two eggs and a strand of hay that fluttered through the bedroom window and landed on my wife's forehead. There are answers to all the unanswered phone calls in this letter. I am not in the letter that I'm not sending because I'm over there reaching for the mailbox. I am reaching from Pennsylvania to childhood and I might dislocate both of my arms.

Keystone Ode with Jane Doe in It

So she didn't have anything
wrapped around her throat
So she didn't have a brass
lump instead of a heart
So her breasts were gone
So her right eye was a bullet
So she did have a toe tag
So her fingers dug a tunnel
So her name is Dirt
So there was a witness
So she did build a fire
So it wasn't enough
to make it out alive
So her girlfriend was murdered
So her grocery list blew away
So she didn't go to buy milk
So the wind inside her throat
activated a blessing
So the Appalachian Trail
is her gravesite
So she was a lesbian
So she swallowed a peach pit
So she did stay on the trail
So the crickets
sound like can openers
So little shards of metal
dig into flesh
So there are bears
and sandwich meat
and chewed fingernails
So there's a forest
with broken crickets
So it sounds like a leaky faucet
So all women are sinners
fixing the rainbow

So this is the sermon
So in the last scene
a white man waves
at the camera
in the background
everything empties out

Keystone Ode with Moving Violation in It

The spare tire in the trunk
is flat. The rubber is rotting;
it's covered with deer guts and my guts
and my grandmother's fingerprints.

On the way to heaven
I'll probably get pulled over
by the cops. I'll scratch the blue
paint and try to pick the lock.
My ride will break down near a volcano
that looks like a giant boob.

Stranded and thirsty, I ache for one
last taste of this life, dump my shame
in the trunk of a 1989 Dodge Dart
and trespass through cornfields.
Out here in the middle of Pennsylvania
there are no corners to turn.

from The Book of Dirt

If I'm a wife   and my wife is a wife
who vacuums the house   and cleans the dishes
which wife dusts   and which one does laundry

who cleans the dirt   off of the dirt
which one of us sucks dirt and which one spits out dirt
which one of us doesn't fit into the word   *wife*

if *wife* is carved   into the dirt   whose left breast
falls off   and whose right eye is dug out
if the wind   is prayer   if dirt is 50% lesbian

and 50% void   if it never rains   how do mosquitoes
suck the gay out   if we live below ground
in our dirt house   do we get squatters' rights

can we sue the land   if the land is our witness   if
we inhale the earth   if our bodies   are silent
tell us what we own   if the law of the dirt

is dirt   if wives travel west   of the dirt
what customary law influences   property rights
if individual grains   of sediment   never move

if the force of gravity   pulls us deeper   into the dirt
if there's no gust   of wind   or   water   or   ice
our marriage will never   sculpt itself   into a mountain

if the valley of dead-women-in-the-dirt   has been
our destination this whole time   all we had to do
was walk   barefoot   in   our   backyard

Keystone Ode with Lesbian Car in It

My life kept
a yellow nylon
rope in the
trunk and the
windows rolled up.
It drove to
the liquor store,
looked for a
new life, drank
a gallon of
oil, wore out
the brakes, swallowed
mouthful after mouthful
of gasoline. My
life left the
radio on, drained
the battery. I
abandoned the two-
door stick shift
when the floor
rotted and my
lungs started to
rust. My life
stalled at every
red light. It
was impounded. My
radiator leaked and
the head gasket
exploded. My life
corroded. I scrubbed
it with baking
soda and a
toothbrush. My wedding
ring fell into
the engine. Damn.

Red State

Sometimes streetlamps flicker
outside of my bathroom window.
Old hallucinations rattle out of my left eye
and my dead body trickles out of the other.
Sometimes I wake up from a drunk dream,
it smells like dandelions in wet dirt. Sometimes
I dig deeper into the dream and my brain falls
into a barrel of wine. I splash. Convince myself
to stay in the holy water until I ferment.
If I do get out alive it costs me my lungs,
both my hands, at least one leg, my eyesight,
and my tongue. It takes   all my breath.

Sometimes I wake up from a drunk dream,
my fingers stained red. I must have scratched
my legs all night as if I could scrape my way out
of this disease. I take a shower, get dressed,
change the sheets, then check my email.
Every message says that I didn't drink the wine,
that it guzzled me. Just before sunrise
the streetlamps stop flickering. A dog barks,
a garbage truck drives by. It's Tuesday,
July 19. I hurtled out of sleep to get here.

Every so often I hitchhike in a dream,
alone on the side of the road. I wait
and wait. I'm in the distance looking
for what's left of a car accident from
the night before last. A shredded tire,
shortness of breath, a shirtsleeve
torn in half. I expect to find a shoe
in the tall grass. There are always
so many shoes on the side of the road.
Every time I get to this part of the dream
I wake up. It's like I take my whole body off,
so that I don't get lost in the wreckage.

Notes from the Commonwealth

The cuts on my heels sting
from walking barefoot through news headlines.

Just yesterday, I fell in love. I fell on the sidewalk.
I fell into a pile of jackknives.

I've been soaking my feet
in a bucket of rocks for fifteen years.

My arms and legs and feet wrapped in gauze.
Layers of skin, wads of crumpled dollar bills, newspapers,

toilet paper tucked into my sleeves and socks—
I mean, I held my wife's hand when we went for a walk

and someone threw rocks at us, then someone else threw glass,
then a soda can, then a styrofoam cup full of ice.

It was a Sunday morning. No, a Tuesday.
It was a Friday when we pretended to hold hands.

We dreamed that nothing could cut us apart—
not the knives, not the news, not the gravel.

It was a Wednesday. The traffic was slower than usual—
at the crosswalk we waited for the light.

We waited for all of the light, but we were looking
down instead of up. We were looking for a softer,

silent rock or a saint or a rabbi.
We searched the cracks in the road and found dust.

We picked up handfuls of soot and worshipped
the street corner. In this town, wind and rocks

and arms and feet fight like red-tailed hawks;
every time we hold hands, prayer happens.

Keystone Ode with Overgrown Garden and Invasive Species in It

The wisteria crawling
out of our kitchen faucet
probably won't flower
for another twenty years.
Lilac will eventually blind us.

We sleep with the carbon
flowers and lipstick plants,
shedding body parts
as they do. The rubber
tree's roots reach
into the sewer system.

What does it mean
to survive? Basil bursting
out of sidewalks?
The choking plant
turning blue? The foot plant
kicking us to death?

At sunrise, we mistake
baby's breath for fog;
it grows around our necks,
pulls the lesbian out
of our dirt. We leave behind
skin and bone wrapped
in wool. We almost

survived the shape of a man.
Lavender grows out of our mouths;
it swells between our cracked breastbones.
Our guts tender and fertile.

Keystone Ode with Homophobia and Ground Beef in It

I'll never fully swallow the bullets, but I'll suck their heat,
cut out a mouth hole for a future generation—

"Don't touch the tomatoes,"
is what I'd say to a thirteen-year-old lesbian.
"Taste them with your eyes closed, or open;
they are ripe red breasts."
I always get wrong what is right.

Who will sell the guts of this life
splayed next to fistfuls of boob?

What I am is not on your list of sins.
I am a package of ground beef
dropped in the middle of Pennsylvania.

Fuckingfaggot hangs over the body.
Dykesissyhomo seeps into the pavement.

This is how the *guntothetemple* says Hail Mary.
No queers get out of here alive.
Fathers rub the crotch of their pants
to compensate for fabric softener.
Mothers toss their children under the bellies
of rainbows mistaken for butchered meat.

Hunger is against us. Whole families
eat the voices baked into the bread.
What I am is not on your grocery list—
cherry tomatoes, bullets, tumors, dinner rolls.
Beef...scattered in a grocery store parking lot.

Bitchtown, Pennsylvania

The Town of Bitch has one grocery store, one coffee shop, one hospital, and one library. All the residents of Bitchtown wake up early and drink Bitch Coffee (the coffee beans are from Bitches County). The bitches go to the grocery store and fill their carts with cans of Bitch Food. They stop off at the hospital to visit their old, bitch mothers. Then they go to the library and read about how to grow a bitch from scratch. By the time they get home it is time to cook dinner, and by nightfall everyone in Bitchtown is lying in bed counting bitches. They fall asleep and dream only bitch dreams.

Notes from the Commonwealth

I want to be the chicken in the front seat of that Cadillac
driving down Route 11. The chicken that reaches
for the steering wheel when there's another chicken
in the road. The chicken that changes a flat tire
and the chicken that doesn't get beat up for loving
other chickens. I want to be the red feathered chicken
with white feathered chicks. The chicken with big breasts
that doesn't wear a bra. The chicken that can actually fly;
I'd soar over Pennsylvania, over cornfields,
and over the prison. I'd free caged chickens
and dig graves for dead chickens.
I'd tie a dollar to a string and catch the guards
who guard jailed chickens. I'd wear my human costume,
patrol the highways, and pull over chicken trucks.
Maybe I want to be a chicken because a chicken's
life is short; a chicken's panic is usually caged.
Maybe I am chicken when I don't hold my wife's hand
at the movies or on a walk through town. I'm chicken
when I pull my arm off her shoulder after someone
whispers, *eww, homos*. Chicken feathers have taken over
my face and skin and courage. I'm the chicken
craning my neck through bars and the chicken
with a broken beak.

Red State

I'm afraid of what the world will do if the other 49 bullets
are in the president's mouth. If they are tossed
like stones that skip across Florida. If the other 49 bullets
sink to the bottom of our country, if our pulse rate rises.
If hearts explode, if bullets sit in our intestines,
or pass through our kidneys.

I'm afraid of what the world will do if the other 49 bullets
are in the trunk of a car. If they are headed to the hospital.

If the other 49 bullets are in pavement. In vinyl house siding.
In brick. In the flesh of the innocent. In the soles of shoes.
In quadriceps. In groins. In necks. In bladders. In spleens.
In throats. I'm afraid if the other 49 bullets are bullets.

from The Book of Dirt

The cows and apple trees and tractor trailers
thump between the prison yard and the university.
Sometimes I chase a herd of cows out of my classroom
and the earth thumps. The word of the lord thumps.
The word thump breaks my ribs. Brown, battery-operated
cows thump through traffic. Factories thump and farmers
thump. The warehouses are full of thumps. The sky thumps
to the ground when I get home from work and kiss my wife.
When two women fall asleep in the same bed
the stars thumpthumpthumpthumpthump
like bullets hovering over our heads.

from **The Book of Dirt**

There's a guy
who looks like
my Uncle Mike
standing
on the corner
of Hanover
and High St.
He reaches
down
his pants
and pulls
out
a long
skinny poem—
he gets arrested.
The handcuffs
are too tight.
Plaid shirts
hang on flagpoles,
sneakers clog the sewers,
the purslane is wilting,
and my radishes
are in a bunch.
It's noon;
the farmer's market
closes in an hour.
Honey, we better be on our way.

from The Book of Dirt

In the dirt where I come from,
there are rocks like men and men with rocks
who drop out of earth to sell pussy
for fifty cents a pop.

They call the dirt dead,
the stones faggots,
the rotting tree roots homos.
They call the women dead
and dirt falls out of their ears.
The dead dirt listens
to the queers. Your dirt is dead, too.

There's no more room in earth.
Buckets of dirt pile into the back
of police cars. On the way to the station
we hit every dead end. These underground
roads are blessed by decay.

At the bottom of love
there's a pile of rocks.
I've been digging to get here.
The gay between my fingers
rubs until I am dust again.

This rock, this one rock,
is the gayest of them all.
She was polished, then
tossed into the river.

Keystone Ode with Assault Rifle and Grocery List in It

There are fruit-shaped guns
at the supermarket:
the apples have triggers,
the avocados, bullets,
the extra, large barrel-bananas
are discounted on Tuesday
when you buy two bunches.
The grenades are nestled
next to the black grapes
and the green grapes
explode on impact.
Once a month
there's a "Blowback" sale
and day-old fruit-guns
are free after 7 p.m.
I can't face it:
we are running low on
apple-shaped apples
and avocado-shaped avocados.
The handgun-oranges,
AR-15-grapefruits,
and pistol-pomelos
are always two hundred dollars off
in the weekly flyer.
The corn in aisle nine pops
when you pay
with your NRA Visa.
In the gun-shaped produce section
there's a raffle
for the 20-gauge-melon-
pump-action with a 26-inch barrel.
To enter, all you have to do
is show up and say, *I hate gays.*

Notes from the Commonwealth

Although I am on a diet from death
I am that abandoned warehouse
next to the farm and all the leftover inventory.

I am the broken hands and broken heads
working at the Lindt Chocolate Factory.
I am stuck in traffic.

I am the fake gold chain
hanging around my brother's neck
and I am an unanswered phone call.

I am a long drive on Route 81
and all the cows in the field
that breathe car exhaust.

I am chewing through an electric fence.
Meanwhile, a beating heart breaks
into my house and the neighbors think I am dead.

Keystone Ode with Hot Sauce and Motor Oil in It

I live between a Kentucky Fried Chicken
and a Red Devil gas station,
between panic and pregnant teenagers,
between the Turnpike and Route 81.
The off-ramps twist like obstructed intestines
and the elephants at the tollbooth toss quarters,
make a wish, then head to the sex shop or truck wash.
These elephants get dizzy on their way to the elephant parade
that stops in front of my house on Sunday mornings.

A blue elephant with orange wisps of hair
stops at the Red Devil to fill up on red and devil.
He litters—there's a pile of needles on the side of the road.
This beast tosses everything in the gutter
with chicken bones, hope, sour beef,
respiratory disease, and underfunded schools.

Bitchtown, Pennsylvania

Some bitch like me sets the fire, cranks
the heat, burns the toast, swallows the flare.

The flowerpots and front lawns blaze
one little fire at a time. Flames sprout
from the gardens on Hanover Street.
Yellow fires and red fires and motherfuckers
drive trucks that are on fire. The chicken hut,
gas station, post office, and the neighbors: all on fire.

When the train passes through this neighborhood of flames
a gust of wind knocks over the bitch who lit the first match.
Her fire burns on fear. Pretty soon the black sky
swirls in flames and the clouds shrivel up,
dry out, and drop like dog shit

to the sides of the streets and highways
where heroin addicts are left for dead, where farmers
grow lettuce and trade sheep for shoelaces and guns,
where starving cows are auctioned
and eaten alive, and the people

confuse women for beef and love for needles.

Keystone Ode with Marianne Moore in It

Marianne Moore Was Here (1896-1916)
Carlisle, Pennsylvania

Near the train tracks
and Chen's Chinese Restaurant,
there's a blue and gold plaque with your name on it,
a row of houses for sale, a man pushing a tin baby
in a canopy stroller, and a boysenberry bush in bloom.
On Tuesdays the train passes,
frightens the stray cats.
The sewage system
grows old inside the belly of this town,
where contaminated water drives a wedge of iron
through Pennsylvania history.
The snails are Dutch, the slugs are French,
and a steamroller passes while men
crush the bones of Carlisle,
while the ghosts of confederate soldiers
and Ohio Indians separate us,
while salesmen suck me in
to the line of traffic on Route 11,
while the shape of your face and tricorne hat
hang in a plume of exhaust trailing from tailpipes—
there are hundreds of pots and pans
stacked on the back of a truck
idling in front of my house.

from The Book of Dirt

There's a cricket trapped on the opposite side of the house
where I hung on a metal hanger
next to all my father's wool coats.
Where I used to pickpocket emptiness,
search for spare change. The back of the coat closet
is where dogs die and gay teenagers never settle.
The cricket crunches like a can opener
and scraping metal reminds me
of teeth grinding—teeth my teenage self
swallowed when I tried to outrun the police;
the teeth I spit like rocks into a lake
when I regurgitated all the L's in Lesbian.

I used to skip rocks across water with my father.
Small flat stones bounced like prayers
before they sank. In the background,
an orchestra without violins or cellos.
Behind the orchestra barbed wire wraps
around a warehouse full of recalled patio furniture.
Millions of swivel patio chairs posed as a fall hazard
all across the country. Entire families and neighborhoods
of betrayal fell out of their chairs onto the dirt
next to charred steaks on the grill. Backyards full of picnics
and dogs choking on their leashes. Some of these dogs
curled up in a corner of shade and chewed off a leg.
Eventually, they ran, three-legged, into the warehouses
filled with piles of aluminum chairs—I confused
clanking metal for crickets.

Keystone Ode with *The House of Mirth* in It

Heaven is an expensive house with fine linens,
creamy butter, and a staff of maids and butlers
who leave coffee stains on the furniture
in the shape of a boot.

I imagine Edith Wharton holding a doily
at the gates of heaven, or maybe she is the doily
in the afterlife. And Lily Bart is on a fainting couch
having an affair with my wife
while I'm grooming the dog that looks like a cloud
in the shape of a doily. I'm worried that I might
menstruate in heaven because I died before
menopause.

Two women live in an old brick house
with an electric oven and a white dog.
At night they howl at the moon
before it is new again.

The women bake bread and brush the dog
in preparation for their entrance into heaven.

Notes from the Commonwealth

Dead Woman's Hollow Road: Cumberland County, Pennsylvania

You watch the news to find out that lesbians don't wash away
after drinking dirt, that the dirt didn't absorb all the rain last week,
that there's everything to name and no voice to repair the rainbow,
that the history of queer was murdered in the Michaux State Forest.
I heard about the woman who ran from the echo of hate—one shot at a time.
I mean, I went to the grocery store, bought mushrooms covered in dirt,
rinsed their white heads, poured olive oil on them, the news in the background.
There's a storm coming, a flood warning, maybe a murderer on the loose. I cooked
and swallowed dirt. Eleven miles away a tree named Rebecca sank into the land.

I am on the other side of the rainbow in the dirt
that doesn't make the news: lesbians sprout like wild strawberries;
their root systems tangle with murder. In Pennsylvania, crushed bones
cut into the land, and daughters collapse before they are auctioned off
every Sunday morning. This ritual is for sale in the church parking lot
where blessings smell like gunfire, and fingers break the sound barrier
as they dig for life.

The dirt under the dead woman's fingernails: sacred.
The yeast in her throat: scooped out, melted down,
and served as communion.

Red State

What if in your dream
you went hunting without a gun
or maybe you are a bear that lives
behind an elementary school
where teachers teach magic
where teachers teach dreams
where teachers teach you how to pray
to gods named Nin, Shara, Maria, Jan,
Lucille.

What if in your dream there was a classroom
full of men and women who shot bullets
out of their eyes. What if books were murdered
this way. If our eyes evolve into guns that shoot
at every single word. What if.

What if this is a silent poem that lives on King Street
in small-town Pennsylvania, and you saw its
silhouette in the window. What if your eyes shot
a stream of bullets, and this poem's wife
was sitting on the sofa, too. You've just killed
me, my wife, and a stray bullet killed the farmer
who farms corn down the road. What if
your eyes won't stop shooting
when you are at the drive-thru
on your way home from work. Your eyes
open fire at the menu and maim all the pink meat.

Pink meat splatters on roads, smears
across windshields. Tractor trailers
drive through pink slime, birds make
nests with it. The sky turns pink. What if.
Air Force One crashes into a cloud of pink meat
on its way to Russia and the president's hair
floats across the ocean and washes ashore

on Brighton Beach. What if. After you rode
the Wonder Wheel, you stood in line
for a hotdog, and there was a strand
of orange hair in the mustard.

Keystone Ode with Founding Father in It

First Presbyterian Church: Carlisle, Pennsylvania
"George Washington worshipped here in 1794."
10 a.m. Worship: life now and in the world to come.

George, this worship has bullet holes in it—
Reverend Myers sent me and Charles Salyards
to loosen the noose, to empty the fire extinguisher,
to dip our hands in holy water, and to say,
"rejoice" and "glory" and "get your hand out of my pocket."
And you say, "why? I need money."

This prayer is interrupted by another prayer.
Trucks and motorcycles have been unleashed on earth.
Reverend Myers is in the front row of the balcony.
Just up the road, an officer writes a parking ticket,
and I can't tell if you are in prison or if it is me.

Truck exhaust smears the stained glass windows
and I can't hear the organ player's tune;
we need to sing faster, to march single file,
to lower our voices from the balcony
and our bodies from these cell blocks.
All of us won't fit through the iron bars.
Maybe we'll have to set the floor planks on fire
and escape through the smokescreen,
or maybe we can hide under a blanket and collect dust
until 10 a.m. service starts on a Sunday in 2094.

from The Book of Dirt

Carlisle, Pennsylvania

We destroyed everything—
read the book about lesbian sex
and the one about how to be a gay dad.

We destroyed everything—
the Shawnee Indians and restricted
sale of rum and whiskey.

We destroyed women,
Captain Williams, wool blankets,
the ceramic librarian stamping books.

We destroyed the grocery store aisles
stocked with tomato juice. We die
in some small way standing in line at the post office.

We destroyed the portrait of that "Carlisle Gentleman"
by untying his tie, unbuttoning his shirt, removing the book
from his right hand, and shaving his widow's peak.

We need to repurpose the wood from the floorboards,
take off the black straitjackets, and donate a dollar
to the Don Quixote exhibit on the first floor.

Notes from the Commonwealth

The Normal School
Shippensburg, Pennsylvania

Somewhere inside this office there's a desk with a door
and a man with a key. Behind the door there's a ladder
and a paint can and a tree. Inside this tree the headmaster wears
a shadow on his head. It drapes over his face. The students
are trained to translate Indian songs and train whistles
and cloud shapes. There are wooden wheels and soldiers marching
through this school. There's an army that has already lost
and another army that laid down on the grass: all the soldiers fake their deaths.
They'll never stop breathing and the schoolboys will paint them white,
plant grass, lay brick, export human hearts and rabbit meat—fuel for future war.

Notes from the Commonwealth

Chandler's poem about a gold chain
is a sinker on a fishing line
in the classroom where fluorescent
lights suck smoke out of my lungs.
Smoke that I inhaled 20 years ago
is falling out of my mouth,
it smears the chalkboard.
This smoke was lodged behind my voice box.
I turn the lights off and barbed wire appears,
it cuts my desk in half and stops me
from telling Chandler that I don't know
what to do about the man in Wyoming who got fired
for being gay—*we can't stop being gay.*
After class I buy apples from an Amish stand
on Route 11 and feel silenced.
God regurgitated the batch of apples
I brought home to my wife.
She made me a pie.

from The Book of Dirt

Tractors plow through pastures
every day. I call my mother on the potato
and somewhere in the earth there are more potatoes—
at the center of every potato is the sound of nothing.
The same nothing that my mother prays
for on long winter nights like this one.

The sky hangs over our phone call
like beef in a freezer, minus the head, hooves, viscera,
lungs, and heart. We talk about how warm air blows
out of train stations in New York City
and wonder if Lenny will evaporate and shrivel
as clouds of train breath linger.

In most potatoes, there's a fist of terror. The same terror
that wakes my father in the middle of the night.
Is he having night terrors about Lenny again? I ask her.

We pray for nothing
between potatoes and cow shit,
between a mother's fingers and a son's toes,
between the streets I roam in small-town Pennsylvania,
where horses puff through their giant nostrils
as they pull entire families through winter.

Before we hang up the phone a horse trots
by me, slips on the road, and breaks a leg.
I don't say it, but I worry if the drugs bit off my brother's life.
If his toe is tagged. If there are mashed potatoes
crusting over in a pot in my mother's kitchen sink. If
I will hear the gunshot that takes the horse out of its misery.

Keystone Ode with Local Journalism and the Associated Press in It

After reading The Patriot Newspaper *on July 14, 2015*

The news headlines are stuffed in exhaust pipes
and King Street is about to explode in Shippensburg.
Tailpipes are clogged with the "Military's Transgender Ban"
and the "Number of Uninsured" has hit
the bottom of the Susquehanna.
I am driving on the river bottom
looking for lead musket balls with teeth marks,
something to bite down on while my muffler
burns out and my catalytic converter suffocates.
There are soldiers brushing their hair with bones
down here. My windows are rolled up
while saw blades, British copper half pennies,
and clay marbles float to the surface.
The obituary page is on the shoreline
in a pile of flint and pink arrowheads.
Margaret Mosier Balaban is survived
by thirteen children. She loved to savor
nut roll, raspberry torte, and chocolate
layer cake—her degree in chemistry
was burnt in the oven back in December 1945.
She would have been 91 this year,
but now Mrs. Balaban
is a sheet of paper on the riverbank
where heroin addicts topple over.
This trash pit will never get dug up
and archived because all the historians
are starving to death in toothpick forts.

Notes from the Commonwealth

At 10 a.m. a housewife rips open
a blue and silver can of anchovies
then spits on the sidewalk.
Ten feet away
men from the gas company
stand on steel plates,
and flecks of white paint chip
off row houses,
littering the housewife's front porch.
The shadows of Mack trucks
flash through the living room.
Her hair, like grease from the underbelly
of an engine, glistens in the sunlight.
This, I say, this is what I want
when I imagine myself
longing for freedom.

Red State

Over here, desk drawers have normal desk things in them.
There's nothing other than a stapler and prayers
for rotted teeth falling out of a crack addict's mouth
for what violates the land
for the skunk that sprays my hair
for the homeless version of me
for the homophobic version
for the kiss with no feet that singed my shirtsleeves
for the paper throat that my twelve-year-old self
hid in a notebook when she sat in the back of a classroom.

Sleet and chalk hollowed out my veins
and thick beams of light tunneled under my skin
until the scabs fell off. I'm over here now,
my hands unfold the past / pluck moons from the other side.

I'm not in the dirt knocking on rock
to see if you are home. Over here, there's mud
on my feet and tornadoes spilling out of my guts.
Over here, the dishes are clean, the silverware doesn't blister
or cut through blood vessels. The small, green scars
between my toes curing like anchovies packed in salt.

Notes from the Commonwealth

Escape has failed the people I love.
My brother is cutting off his circulation,
my mother is trapped in a plastic bag, and my father
is held hostage at the Richmond International Airport,
but he gets on the next flight anyway and makes it home
only to find that the dog peed on the kitchen floor,
to find me locked in the garage, revving the car
and filling the place with smoke.

Keystone Ode with Visiting Hours in It

My brain is leftover cake in the freezer.
It's trapped in a Ziploc bag
and if the freezer ever stops freezing
my cake brain will melt.
The chocolate frosting looks like blood
and this bag of brains begins to rot.
My brain is cold out here in Pennsylvania
where black and white gunshots
echo above the train tracks,
where trains carry boxes full of hearts
past the prison... where I sit now
with Rashanya and Elizabeth and Chelsea
in a cold cinder block room
wearing red shirts and pants.
We heat up Pennsylvania from behind bars.

from **The Book of Dirt**

I suppose it is just habit
when I grab a chair
and scoot up to the table

I suppose I live in a cornfield
I suppose I'm under
my brother's childhood bed

I suppose his bed
isn't a cardboard box
I suppose there are mashed potatoes

and my brother at the table
I suppose the yellow ceramic bowl is hot
when I pick it up and burn my fingers

I suppose I dig little graves
I mean dig for potatoes
I mean there's no dinner on the table

and there's no brother sitting next to me
and no chairs in the kitchen
and no corn in the fields

and there's no way to imagine
what it was like to survive
ninety days and nights

on wet cement
the floor in prison
is mopped three times a day

from The Book of Dirt

God is a worm,

but not the one baking in the sun at the bus stop
or the worm that my brother made me eat when I was 7.
This worm has never been cut in half.
It doesn't come out when it rains.
The worms in New York and the ones in Pennsylvania
are related to God and sometimes I smell them in a drinking glass
fresh out of the dishwasher. I swear that the difference between
the worm that is God and the worms that live in our guts
has made me regurgitate my desire to drink, swallow it again, then recite
Emily Dickinson, but in my recitation, I get the words wrong.
Instead of a narrow fellow in the grass, there's something
narrow and sly in my pants.

Red State

If I ever lose a fingernail
when I peel a carrot
I will stick my head in the oven,
maybe pour bourbon on my hair and neck,
marinate myself so I really light up.
There will be no reason to call
the medics. They are already upstairs
with the brothel owner, Bessy Jane Jones.

If I ever lose my marriage
I'll know to look for the spare
covered in plastic
hanging in the back of the closet.

If I ever lose my sobriety
I'll look on the riverbank
for a pair of tan boots
and dark blue jeans,
or I'll look under a bus.

Keystone Ode without Jaywalking in It

At the courthouse
June 5, 2015: Carlisle, Pennsylvania

The tombstones in the public square vibrate.
The traffic lights flash brown and blue
on the corner of Hanover and High.
Ben Franklin's face is in the cement;
the brown light reburies the dead Ohio Indians
and the blue competes with the clouds.
Kira and I wait to cross the street,
we touch bullet holes, climb to the top
of the courthouse, and we jump.

Notes from the Commonwealth

I wait for monsters to grab my ankles,
to fold me in half and take my wallet.
The monster in Mark's poem waits
under the Walnut Street bridge.

I wait for monsters to crawl
out of my lungs
and force me to drink
warm cans of beer,
to take me back to where I belong.

I wait for the mail
as if one day I will get my death certificate,
or paperwork from the government
requesting my signature—
my application to get out of hell
has been denied.

I wait in traffic for silence
as trains pass through my lower intestines.

I wait for my alcoholism to kill me
on days like this and federal holidays
and Tuesdays and Sundays,
on days when I don't bother to make the bed,
on days when one of my students puts
a monster in his poem and doesn't let it out.

from The Book of Dirt

I can't tell the difference
between what's dripping from the gutter
and what's dripping from the corner of my mouth
onto the pale green kitchen counter.

There's a dead foot, or mouse,
or just a piece of provolone
that fell behind the stove.
Milk splattered on the wall
next to the fridge.

Sour sweat runs down my face.
Murder bakes at 475 degrees.
Both racks in the oven are about to collapse.

Father must be getting home from work
any minute now. The wall phone next to the sink
rings. Mother's ghost arrives to answer it.

from The Book of Dirt

There were little girls
in the train yard
the night it exploded.
Charcoal, shoes, and fingers
smash into apartment buildings
and mothers mistake
this sound for the furnace.
They toss their child's hand
into the embers, fuel the fire
for the long December night ahead.
This is the kind of story I imagine
my great-grandmother Kutz
telling me over a 7UP float
on a Saturday afternoon as we crank
the ceramic music box,
let the music unwind.
The tinkering sounds
clean the air.

Keystone Ode to My Wife after Reading Anne Bradstreet at a One-Hundred-and-Three-Year-Old Farmhouse

Between two clouds
and two seedless grapes
and two dandelions,
there are days that fall.
Between two horses
or two farm dogs
or two blackbirds,
there is breath.
Between two mice
or two lightning bugs
or two blades of grass
or two fallen crab apples,
there is a silent place to love.
Between two yellow wildflowers
or two fox kits or two red oak leaves,
there is energy that crashes.
Between two frogs and two trees,
there are two rain drops and two gusts of wind
that blow through darkness,
where two stars
and two far away planets
light up the sky.

.

Notes from the Commonwealth

Carlisle, Pennsylvania

If the mortar in this stone wall doesn't melt
and the guard, with toilet paper stuck to his shoe,
doesn't shoot, we'll have nothing to write about
when this building is landmarked.

"Stone wall built in 1757
and in June of 1854 a spider
crawled through the iron bars,
bit a prisoner's eyelid. He was hanged
in the summer of 1860. His face was swollen.
When it rains, his last words seep out
of the mortar. It is said that the rats
knew a way out but never left.
The spiders spun webs above the sinks,
fell into the toilets, but never
drowned."

Keystone Ode with Litter and Exhaust in It

chicken wire and cheesecloth
forks and spoons
and spoons
newspaper and trashcans
pigeons and dumpsters
hangers and condoms
money clips and quarters
on the corner of King and Queen
pickup trucks peel
out of the gas station parking lot

barns and flashlights
gasoline and hay barrels
soup cans and soup cans
tractor trailers and sour apples
human trafficking and empty bathrooms
chocolate factories that melt sugar
and glaze horseshoes
and needles
dripping and sweaty meat
like an empty body
there are too many bodies emptying out
on this road of heroin and alcohol
and beef and hate and forgiveness

from The Book of Dirt

Jesus Jesus Jesus
Janice Rosalia
Father Tauer
blood of St. Francis.

The saints go marching by
and little Jimmy
sits on the sidewalk
naming the ants—George Washington,
Stuart, Captain James,
Ernest, White Thunder.
He aims his magnifying glass
at the ant carrying
a piece of hotdog bun
until it catches fire.

Little Jimmy swallowed
fire when he pulled
Peggy's hair in math class.

This kind of worship
repeats itself,
and there is a sweet potato
in the microwave
about to explode.

Red State

I was in his house. The dog was in the closet.
I found his bones, named him Charlie,
then searched the kitchen drawers.
I read the mail, turned on the faucet
and gazed at the backyard.
Brown water and roaches on my hands and feet.
I pushed myself into the future,
into the linen closet, into pants' pockets and ashtrays.
I always find other drug addicts who suffered,
choked, swallowed a rotting mouthful of milk.
I'm worried about the emptiness on the kitchen table.
If I could fit another drug addict inside of me
I'd siphon one out of my brother
through the corner of his eye.
There's relief in that plant on the windowsill.
I'll name her Ms. Bart,
give her a drop of water.

from The Book of Dirt

Sometimes I live in a cornfield
with scarecrows that wear helmets.
Sometimes I live in a box of cereal or in a barn.
I have giant sacs of milk that need to be squeezed.
Sometimes I ride a tractor and collect eggs.
Sometimes I roll bales of hay in the pasture
where blue and brown cows shit blue and brown.
Sometimes I relive the first time I drank too much
and wake up under a car
in the middle of a busy road
and in the distance a farmer
strips cornstalks and drops
ears into a bucket.

Notes from the Commonwealth

If I were a sweet potato in the microwave about to explode
I'd shout, *WATCH OUT,* and then let the dog
lick the floor and walls. I'd ask a neighbor for a mop
and I'd call my mother to tell her that I've finally reached my limit.
I'd crawl on my hands and knees to look for my ring finger,
to see if my wedding ring survived the explosion.

from **The Book of Dirt**

Say tomorrow doesn't come,
and no one opens the cupboard

to get the salt and pepper and pancake mix.
If I'm in the kitchen cupboard,

and tomorrow doesn't come
breakfast won't be ready

for the farmer who fell asleep in the cornfield.
No one will find the cow that wandered

into the woods to rot with the apples.
There'll be no one to get the milk.

The farmer's wife broke her neck
instead of the chicken's.

from **The Book of Dirt**

It was like a christening except all the angels
were police, the sign of the cross a drug deal.
Alcoholism wet the bed when I was born.

39 years later hospital beds hang
from tree branches. Rusty metal bedframes
rip alcoholic arms out of their sockets,
and doctors put them in warm beer
to cure root rot.

The day alcoholism took Gerry's life,
his limp, fermented body sank into a blue mattress,
his feet dangled into Tuesday morning.
I wonder if the empty bottles around his body
were recycled. If someone got the five-cent deposit
for his ribcage. If the oak trees suffocated.
If his alcoholic arms and legs will get sober
now that they are in dirt. If the earth is a little
drunk from his bones.

Gerry cracked the instrument of peace,
ate yellow spiders one night,
and never woke up.
His lungs filled with synthetic cotton,
mattress springs, and prayer.

Gerry's dead and I'm not.
He helped me regurgitate a pair of handcuffs.
Gerry's dead. I'm not.
He drove me to a chicken coop once.
Gerry's dead. I'm not.
He introduced me to all the chickens.
Gerry's dead. I'm not.
He drank the holy water
after 20 years of sobriety.
He's dead. I'm thirsty and I'm not.

Alcoholism wet the bed when Gerry died.
It was like a baptism except his second birth
was not an imitation, it soaked through the mattress.

The rocks in Gerry's gut burst—
his dust storm carries a never-ending elegy
to the next drunk in the next town.

Keystone Ode with Prison Dinner in It

I'll remind you to catch the fish before eating it next time
I know it must have smelled good roasting in the fire
but forgetting to light the flame was no help
and stabbing your life with a stake can only taste so good
in your dreams I'll be there standing on one leg
not because I am meditating
but this is all I'll have left
after swimming one thousand miles to get here
one of my legs will have fallen off and washed ashore
where you were left to starve
I was paranoid you'd be alone

Notes from the Commonwealth

It's okay to dig your grandmother
out of her grave, then chop wood
and sit on a log that floats
down the Susquehanna River.
It's okay to stand in mud and pray
to an empty grave,
to call your brother and leave
a message and to never go
looking for him. It's okay
to spend the inheritance money
on the idea of forgiveness
by burying it in the backyard,
then digging it up to take the quarters
for laundry then forgetting
to go to the laundromat.
It's okay that this happened,
that your legacy ends
with a fistful of loose change.

But it's not okay that the butcher
at the grocery store dips spoiled
loins and shanks and T-bones
in blood to boost America's courage.
Grocery boys and cash and imported cheese
and cans of crushed tomatoes—all dipped
in blood. Maybe all those red lips
in the photos of our grandmothers
are fresh blood and the shadows,
rotten meat.

Keystone Ode with Despair and an Unmentioned Avocado in It

Hope is the pomegranate molasses
that I added to the grocery list
on my way out the door.

Hope melts a little on Mondays.
It spoils. The man who works
the hope counter is in the middle
of a divorce and child custody battle.
When he's hungover he forgets to add more ice
to the slices of hope in the display case.
This hope is a little bloody,
a little tart—make sure to coat it in salt.

Hope is on the grocery list that I forgot
on the kitchen counter. I was going to run errands
after I taught a class in prison this afternoon.
The prison guard said, *the poetry lady is here,*
then he unlocked the gate.

from The Book of Dirt

Those were the days I walked
through the Kentucky Fried Chicken parking lot
frying my lungs and muzzling
my imaginary dog named Bucket.
My car was missing a passenger seat
and there was a brown paper bag full of corn
in the trunk. My fingers were as cold as steaks
on the back of a UPS truck.
I always drank to get drunk
and now I want to promise myself
that I can get drunk when I turn 82.
The only thing between me and that promise
is a 122 oz. can of stewed tomato halves.
I'll never open this can
because there's no such thing
as a 122 oz. can of stewed tomatoes
and no such thing as another drunk
     that I'll survive.

Keystone Ode with Environmental Contaminants

I

I'm standing on Front Street
in Harrisburg drinking
nuclear reactor coolant
and shooting radioactive
iodine into my veins.

II

This ain't no place to hide.

III

If we throw everyone in the river
then no one will volunteer
to evacuate.

IV

Dr. Heidegger didn't drink the water.
C.K. Williams drank the water.

V

So much depends upon cows
and soldiers
and the river's edge.
Sometimes we are less
desperate and less alone.

VI

This makes us thirsty
and the fish
in the Susquehanna River
need chemotherapy.

VII

We made it onto CNN.
Wolf Blitzer says,
We are all going to die.

Red State

I'm afraid to look under my neighbor's car.
What if it's me that I find?
What if I drowned in the bathtub last night?
What if I never made it home?

Under my neighbor's car
I'd expect to find a stray cat
or a chicken bone that was tossed
out of a car window in the middle of the night.

In the middle of the night
moons circle my house
tires get slashed
and people hide in the bushes.

In the middle of the night
mailmen get ready to deliver bills and letters
and coupons—any two pizzas with two toppings
for ten bucks—the pizza delivery girl might be
what I find under my neighbor's car.

Keystone Ode with #MeToo in It

So #MeToo cuts her ponytail off, walks into a bar and takes a seat next to #MeToo and the bartender serves #MeToo whiskey from an eyedropper she pulls straight out of her purse, but it turns out #MeToo was already in every purse because #MeToo comes as a picture inside every wallet. #MeToo carries tweezers everywhere she goes, plucks chin hairs before her picture is taken. #MeToo slides into a bra strap, tucks into a sock, falls out of a pocket, folds into a shirtsleeve, gets lost in a discount rack. #MeToo shuts up. Drinks. #MeToo never loses the memory.

#MeToo, like when my high school soccer coach hijacked my shin pads and cleats he drained the water cooler sucked the orange slice out of my mouth the warehouse out of my mind the metal cage out of my lungs the ferris wheel seat that flips inside my gut yes he resigned I was a goalie I wanted to tell his wife wanted to cut his tongue out rip his face off my torso hardened into tree bark when my shirt came off her torso hardened into tree bark when her shirt came off she wanted his wife to yell but it was sunday then tuesday and 16 is hard pavement her head is my head against the curb my hair wrapped around her throat I was 16 I swear I never kissed back

So #MeToo wants to tell his wife, wants his daughter's name not to be Nicole. #MeToo was kicked off the soccer team. He ran for mayor as a democrat, just like #MeToo. So you lost the sour taste of being a teenager, #MeToo? Me too. Now she stands in front of a classroom twenty years later with hair down to her knees and when a student says #MeToo, she imagines her soccer cleats dangling from his rearview mirror as he gags on a wad of her hair.

Notes from the Commonwealth

Wooden wheels crack on pavement,
and a woman flashes her horse.
The leather straps grind
and squeak. The horse sweats.
This is the traffic report today
on Route 11. I wonder if horse sweat
can cure depression or drug addiction
in this part of the country. I follow
this horse and buggy into the Walmart
parking lot. The Amish go to buy aspirin.
While my head throbs, mountains unfold
behind white stone houses every time I drive by.

Every time I drive by mountains or a horse
the pavement cracks. I smell sweaty teenagers
in conversion therapy. I swallow sulfur
as milk trucks pull to the side of the road.
I strike the guardrail and am airborne until
my body slams into dirt. I taste all of the queer
blood drenched in the land. My head throbs.
While concrete barriers circle heaps of hate,
white stone houses crumble and women disappear.
I wonder if crushed stone is like fairy dust,
if it will blind the sexist/homophobic/motherfuckers
just enough to stop them in their tracks.

Keystone Ode with Queer Skin

Now that I am the person under your skin,
I will overcook the green beans
and scrub the stains off your elbows.
I'll go back to 1969. I'll wear metal shoes
and a brown paper bag over my heart.
I'll bolt the bedroom window shut,
tie your feet to the bedposts,
and lock the past in the liquor cabinet.
I'll freeze your heart and lungs
so I can thaw them out
when you're ready to love.

Keystone Ode with Businessmen in It

I heard about how good the pussy is on the market these days.
Men go door to door selling pussy from their briefcases.
Just the other day Dick and his wife, Jane,
started to seriously consider an investment in pussy.
Jane told Dick he's nuts, that pussy loses value,
how it is no different than the depreciation of a car.
She told him that buying into pussy is like buying a coffin
to lay down and take a nap in; Jane's been lying
in her pussy coffin for years.
Sometimes pussy is like a giant hairy taco
that will swallow you whole if your face gets too close.

The pussy truck parks next to the taco truck
at the farmer's market. Jane recommends the pussy
with the white gills, red stem, the one that wears a skirt
and has a bulbous sack. There are men who forage
for pussy in broad daylight. They dig their hands
into the soil and pluck whole pussies from the earth in one grab.
The pussy beneath the soil is not calling to a man
as if he were a thing from the dirt like a tuber.
The pussy that grows at the edge of the woods
is usually on state owned land.
Trespassers walk through the woods,
fill their briefcases, then head straight
to town to ring your doorbell.

Notes from the Commonwealth

In *The Book of Dirt*
there are no gravestones
or shovels,
no shoes
abandoned
on back porches.

In *The Book of Dirt,*
I bury the fight
I had with my wife.
This dirt
is on the dog's feet
and on every window
of our house.
There's dirt
on my apology note
that won't stick
to the refrigerator door.
There's muck
under the stove
and torn pages
from *The Book of Dirt*—
this might be the last piece
of our marriage.

We'll leave this dirt
on the kitchen floor,
and we'll fight over
the dirt on the rake
resting on a slab
of plywood
in the outhouse
where people
used to shit.
I imagine
Marianne Moore
hovering over
this shithole.

On First Having Read *The Book of Dirt*

and loaded the batteries
into the flashlight, I take off my shoes,
put on my skin. My feet listen to the earth.
Gather digging tools and hallow land.
Check the ground for homophobia and women.

Twenty-five rounds of ammunition: dry dirt.
A forest floor, a myth,
where queers get to the other side.
The dirt without grass has no name.
I've walked there picking bones.

First the walnut tree and then hot bullets.
It is black then brown then earth.
My face, our dream, you. Splitting
in half again and again and again.
I can't find my shovel, so I dig for it.

We wake up touching
in the dirt, in the book.
Our hands reaching from under
as if we could actually be together.

The thing I came for is on the other side
of the dirt, but there's no water, or thirst,
or surface, or air, or sun. This is the place
where there's more wreckage. More bodies.

If there was a ladder, I'd climb out of the dirt.
I'd gather courage to reappear and probably
find myself in the middle of Pennsylvania
carrying *An Atlas of the Difficult World*
and a flashlight with dead batteries.

Acknowledgements

Thank you to the editors and staff of the following publications in which many of these poems first appeared, oftentimes in earlier versions and under different titles: *Atlanta Review, Atticus Review, The Boiler Journal, The Cincinnati Review, The Florida Review, Flyway, Free State Review, Lavender Review, Lunch Ticket, Mipoesias Magazine, Out Magazine, Pittsburgh Poetry Review, Poetrybay, Radar Poetry, The Rumpus, The Seventh Wave, Slipstream, SWWIM, Third Point Press, TINGE, The Tishman Review, Zocalo Public Square.*

Thank you, as well, to the editors of the following anthologies for including poems from this collection:

The Best American Poetry 2019. Series Ed. David Lehman. Guest Ed. Major Jackson. Scribner, 2019.

Misrepresented People: Poetic Responses to Trump's America. Eds. María Isabel Álvarez and Dante Di Stefano. NYQ Books, 2018.

Additionally, several poems in this book appeared in the chapbook, *Spoiled Meat* (Headmistress Press, 2018), which was selected by Ching-In Chen as the winner of the Charlotte Mew Prize.

I would also like to express my appreciation to the LGBTQ community, the Cumberland County Prison, Shippensburg University, and the sober community in central Pennsylvania. I am grateful to Mary Meriam and Jayleen Galarza for their support, for making change happen, and for being role models. I am endlessly grateful to my students at Shippensburg University (past, present, and future); my dear friend, Dante Di Stefano, and his family; my friends and colleagues in the English Department at Shippensburg University, especially the creative writing team: Neil Connelly and Kim Van Alkamade; my teachers, especially Maria Mazziotti Gillan and David Lehman; my parents, Len and Linda; and my brother, Len. Special thanks to Stacey Harwood-Lehman, Nin Andrews, and Laura Cronk for supporting my work and for our friendship. Thanks to the powerful female poets who have visited my students and me at Shippensburg University: Jennifer L. Knox, Shara McCallum, Jan Beatty, Yona Harvey, Nin Andrews, Maria Mazziotti Gillan, and Patricia Smith—your voices are forever in the air of this small town. I am grateful for the support and blurbs from Mark Bibbins, Jan Beatty and David Lehman. Thank you, as well, to The Dante Machine.

Thank you to my wife, Deanna Dorangrichia. I admire your art, your dedication, and am forever grateful that we have us—you are my strength.

**Pennsylvania does not legally support
the following LGBTQ issues as of the publication
date of this book.**

HOUSING
State does not prohibit housing discrimination based on sexual
orientation and gender identity.

EMPLOYMENT
State does not prohibit employment discrimination based on sexual
orientation and gender identity.

HATE CRIMES
State does not have a law that addresses hate or bias crimes based
on sexual orientation and gender identity.

PUBLIC ACCOMMODATIONS
State does not prohibit discrimination in public accommodations
based on sexual orientation and gender identity.

SCHOOL ANTI-BULLYING
State does not have a law that addresses harassment and/or
bullying of students based on sexual orientation and gender
identity.

EDUCATION
State does not have a law that addresses discrimination against
students based on sexual orientation and gender identity.

ANTI-CONVERSION THERAPY
This state has no restrictions on so-called "conversion therapy."

The Human Rights Campaign
www.hrc.org

CPSIA information can be obtained
at www.ICGtesting.com
Printed in the USA
FSHW020100050220
56768FS